DISCARD

SUPER BOWL CHAMPIONS
NEW YORK GIANTS

DEFENSIVE BACK
COREY WEBSTER

SUPER BOWL CHAMPIONS

NEW YORK GIANTS

AARON FRISCH

CREATIVE EDUCATION

Published by Creative Education
P.O. Box 227, Mankato, Minnesota 56002
Creative Education is an imprint of The Creative Company
www.thecreativecompany.us

Design and production by Blue Design
Art direction by Rita Marshall
Printed in the United States of America

Photographs by Corbis (Bettmann), Getty Images (Peter
Brouillet, Bill Cummings, Tom Hauck, Jim McIsaac, Al
Messerschmidt, Ralph Morse/Time Life Pictures, NFL
Photos, Robert Riger, George Rose, Matthew Stockman,
Damian Strohmeyer/Sports Illustrated, Rob Tringali/
SportsChrome, Michael S. Yamashita)

Library of Congress Cataloging-in-Publication Data
Frisch, Aaron.
New York Giants / Aaron Frisch.
p. cm. — (Super bowl champions)
Includes index.
Summary: An elementary look at the New York Giants
professional football team, including its formation in 1925,
most memorable players, Super Bowl championships, and
stars of today.
ISBN 978-1-60818-382-1
1. New York Giants (Football team)—History—Juvenile
literature. I. Title.

GV956.N4F75 2014
796.332'64097471—dc23   2013014831

First Edition
9 8 7 6 5 4 3 2 1

WIDE RECEIVER
IKE HILLIARD

PHIL SIMMS / 1979-81, 1982-93

Phil led New York's offense for 14 seasons. He was one of the smartest quarterbacks in the NFL.

TABLE OF CONTENTS

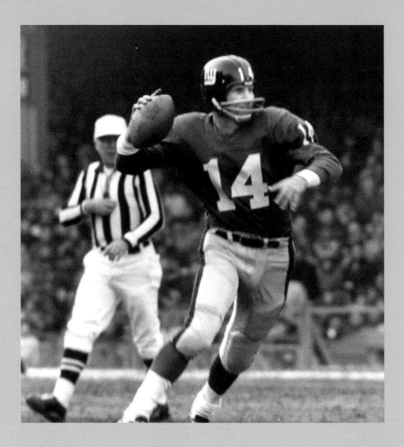

QUARTERBACK
Y. A. TITTLE

THE MIGHTY GIANTS

New York is a giant city. It has huge buildings called **skyscrapers**. It has tall statues and long bridges. New York also has football-playing Giants!

MEL HEIN / 1931–45

Mel was one of the first Giants stars. He was so good that he played both center and linebacker.

4 Times Square

WELCOME TO NEW YORK

New York is home to more than 8 million people. That is more than any other city in America. New York is nicknamed "The Big Apple" and "Gotham City."

FRANK GIFFORD

1952–60, 1962–64

Frank was a fast running back who scored more touchdowns (78) than any other Giants player ever.

ONE TOUGH DIVISION

The Giants play in a tough **division** with three other teams. New York has played a lot of fierce football games against teams called the Cowboys, Eagles, and Redskins.

QUARTERBACK CHARLIE CONERLY

FULLBACK ALEX WEBSTER

CHARLIE CONERLY

"I guess I wouldn't even recognize half the guys I play against in a game if I saw them on the street afterward. They're just a blur when they are coming in at you."
— CHARLIE CONERLY

THE GIANTS' STORY

The Giants started playing in 1925. They won National Football League (NFL) championships in 1927, 1934, and 1938. The Giants had a strong defense with players like tackle Steve Owen.

Quarterback Charlie Conerly helped New York win another championship in 1956. The Giants got to the **playoffs** many times after that.

1934 GIANTS

LAWRENCE TAYLOR

Fast linebacker Lawrence Taylor helped make the Giants great again in the 1980s. The Giants captured Super Bowl trophies after the 1986 and 1990 seasons!

MICHAEL STRAHAN / 1993–2007
Michael was a star defensive end.
In 2001, he set an NFL **record** by
making **22.5 sacks**.

17

WIDE RECEIVER
DAVID TYREE

BILL PARCELLS / 1983-90
Bill was the first Giants coach to win a Super Bowl. His 1986 and 1990 teams won world championships.

he Giants were a good team after that. But they could not win more championships until they added coach Tom Coughlin and quarterback Eli Manning.

After the 2007 season, the Giants beat the undefeated New England Patriots in Super Bowl XLII (42). They beat the Patriots for another championship four years later!

ELI MANNING

In 2013, receiver Victor Cruz caught a lot of passes from Eli Manning. New York fans hoped Victor would help the Giants earn another Super Bowl victory!

VICTOR CRUZ

21

FACTS FILE

CONFERENCE/DIVISION:
National Football
Conference, East Division

TEAM COLORS:
Blue and red

HOME STADIUM:
MetLife Stadium

SUPER BOWL VICTORIES:
XXI, January 25, 1987
    39–20 over Denver
    Broncos
XXV, January 27, 1991
    20–19 over Buffalo Bills
XLII, February 3, 2008
    17–14 over New England
    Patriots
XLVI, February 5, 2012
    21–17 over New England
    Patriots

NFL WEBSITE FOR KIDS:
http://nflrush.com

FAMOUS GIANTS

JASON PIERRE-PAUL / 2010–present

Jason was a fast defensive end. He was very hard to block and loved to chase quarterbacks.

GLOSSARY

division — a group of teams within a league that play many games against each other

playoffs — games that the best teams play after a season to see who the champion will be

record — something that is the most or best ever

sacks — plays in which a defensive player tackles a quarterback who is trying to throw a pass

skyscrapers — tall, narrow buildings that have at least 10 stories, or levels

INDEX